THE AMERICAN LANDSCAPE

NIAGARA FALLS

DWAYNE HICKS

PowerKiDS press

Published in 2026 by The Rosen Publishing Group, Inc.
2544 Clinton Street, Buffalo, NY 14224

First Edition

Editor: Greg Roza
Book Design: Michael Flynn

Photo Credits: Cover, p. 1 Ong.thanaong/Shutterstock.com; (series background) Omeris/Shutterstock.com; p. 5 Edd Lange/Shutterstock.com; p. 7 Radzas2008/Shutterstock.com; p. 9 Ritu Manoj Jethani/Shutterstock.com; p. 11 Blue Cat Studio/Shutterstock.com; p. 13 jiaqing/Shutterstock.com; p. 15 https://commons.wikimedia.org/wiki/File:Chutes_du_Niagara_par_Hennepin.tiff?page=1; p.17 https://commons.wikimedia.org/wiki/File:Westinghouse_Generators_at_Niagara_Falls.jpg; p. 19 https://en.m.wikipedia.org/wiki/File:Queen-of-the-Mist.jpg; p. 21 JHVEPhoto/Shutterstock.com.

Library of Congress Cataloging-in-Publication Data

Names: Hicks, Dwayne, author.
Title: Niagara Falls / Dwayne Hicks.
Description: [Buffalo, New York] : PowerKids Press, [2025] | Series: The American landscape | Includes bibliographical references and index.
Identifiers: LCCN 2024044374 (print) | LCCN 2024044375 (ebook) | ISBN 9781499450927 (library binding) | ISBN 9781499450910 (paperback) | ISBN 9781499450934 (ebook)
Subjects: LCSH: Niagara Falls (N.Y. and Ont.)--Juvenile literature.
Classification: LCC F127.N8 H54 2025 (print) | LCC F127.N8 (ebook) | DDC 971.3/39--dc23/eng/20241030
LC record available at https://lccn.loc.gov/2024044374
LC ebook record available at https://lccn.loc.gov/2024044375

Manufactured in China

Some of the images in this book illustrate individuals who are models. The depictions do not imply actual situations or events.

CPSIA Compliance Information: Batch #QSPK26. For Further Information contact Rosen Publishing at 1-800-237-9932.

CONTENTS

Mighty Waterfall

Niagara Falls is the largest waterfall in North America. It's famous all over the world! About 700,000 gallons (2,650,000 L) of water goes over the falls every second! This world wonder is actually three waterfalls—the Horseshoe Falls, the American Falls, and the **Bridal Veil** Falls.

Horseshoe Falls
Bridal Veil Falls
American Falls

Where Is It?

Niagara Falls is on the Niagara River. This river forms part of the border between the U.S. state of New York and the Canadian **province** of Ontario. The Niagara River connects two of the Great Lakes—Lake Erie and Lake Ontario.

ONTARIO
Toronto
Lake Ontario
Niagara Falls
Niagara River
Buffalo
Lake Erie
NEW YORK

Down the River

Water from the Niagara River falls from 190 feet (58 m) high over Niagara Falls. This rushing water wears away the rocks that make up the falls. This means that the waterfall is slowly moving toward Lake Erie. Thousands of years from now, Niagara Falls will be gone.

Wildlife near the Falls

Although Niagara Falls is a city, it's home to many wild animals. Visitors will see more than 300 kinds of birds, such as Canada geese, owls, and gulls. They will see **mammals** such as deer, rabbits, skunks, and raccoons. They will also find fish such as bass, trout, and more.

gull

Native Americans

Many Native American groups have lived around Niagara Falls. Some of the groups got along and some didn't. One of the earlier groups called themselves the Onguiaahra (ONG-guy-ar-uh). Some people think this is where the name "Niagara River" comes from. Others disagree.

Europeans Arrive

The first European to view the falls was probably French **explorer** Etienne Brule. He told others about what he saw. The first person to see and write a record of Niagara Falls was French priest Louis Hennepin. Many other Europeans made the trip to view the falls, often to draw or paint it.

Power!

In 1895, one of the world's first **hydroelectric** plants was built near the falling water of Niagara Falls. This plant used the power of the falls to make **electricity**. Soon after, nearby Buffalo, New York, became the first city powered by hydroelectricity.

Daredevils!

On October 24, 1901, 63-year-old Annie Edson Taylor went over Niagara Falls in a **barrel** . . . and lived! She was the first daredevil to try this, although the others weren't all as lucky. Today, this is against the law. Daredevils have also walked over the falls using a **tightrope**.

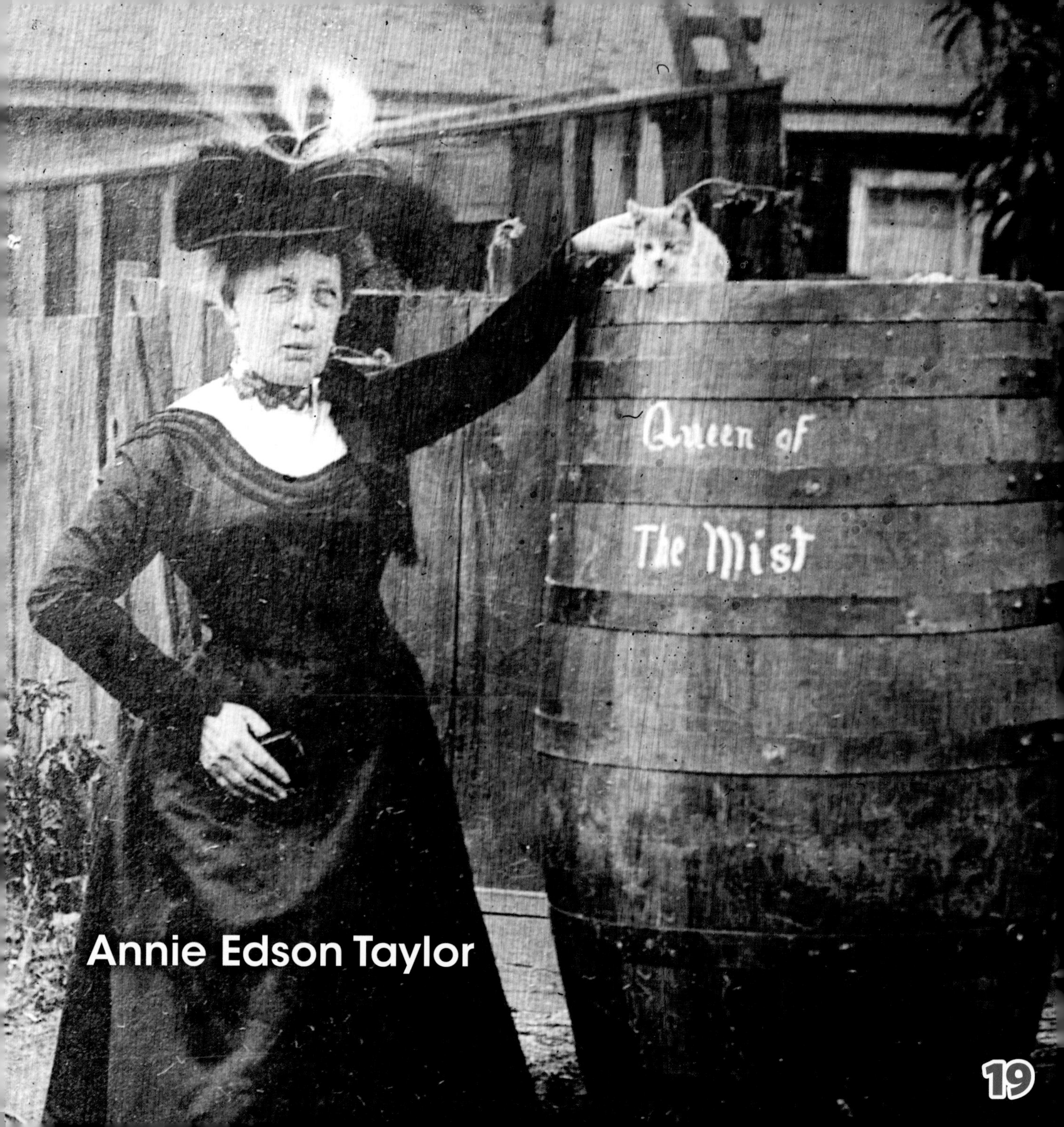

Annie Edson Taylor

Let's Go to Niagara Falls

Today, people who go to Niagara Falls can walk around the falls in New York and Ontario. They can take a ride on a boat called the *Maid of the Mist*. Some people go there to get married! Others go to paint one of the world's greatest wonders.

Maid of the Mist

GLOSSARY

barrel: A large, round keg used to store or ship something.

bridal veil: A long, thin piece of lace commonly worn over the face by women at their weddings.

electricity: A form of energy that flows through wires to reach homes and businesses.

explorer: Someone who searches a place new to them in a careful way to learn more about it.

hydroelectric: Related to the production of electricity using the power of moving water.

mammal: Any warm-blooded animal whose babies drink milk and whose body is covered with hair or fur.

province: Any one of the large parts some countries, such as Canada, are divided into.

tightrope: A rope stretched tight between two points that a trained person can walk on.

FOR MORE INFORMATION

BOOKS

Bolt Simons, Lisa M. *Niagara Falls*. Lake Elmo, MN: Focus Readers, 2018.

Jacobson, Bray. *Niagara Falls*. New York, NY: Gareth Stevens, 2023.

Yazdani, Sheila. *Ontario*. New York, NY: Crabtree Books, 2024.

WEBSITES

Daredevils of Niagara Falls
www.niagarafallslive.com/daredevils_of_niagara_falls.htm
Read more about the daring (and crazy) people who have purposely gone over the falls.

Niagara Falls Live Cam
www.cliftonhill.com/niagara-falls/livecam
Visit this website to view a live cam of the Horseshoe Falls.

INDEX